Uakari

by Julie Murray

Abdo Kids Jumbo is an Imprint of Abdo Kids
abdobooks.com

abdobooks.com

Published by Abdo Kids, a division of ABDO, P.O. Box 398166, Minneapolis, Minnesota 55439.

Abdo Kids Jumbo™ is a trademark and logo of Abdo Kids.

Printed in the United States of America, North Mankato, Minnesota.

102024

012025

Photo Credits: Alamy, Animals Animals, Getty Images, Minden Pictures, Nature Picture Library, Science Source, Shutterstock

Production Contributors: Teddy Borth, Jennie Forsberg, Grace Hansen
Design Contributors: Victoria Bates, Candice Keimig

Library of Congress Control Number: 2024936634

Publisher's Cataloging-in-Publication Data

Names: Murray, Julie, author.

Title: Uakari / by Julie Murray

Description: Minneapolis, Minnesota : Abdo Kids, 2025 | Series: Unusual animals | Includes online resources and index.

Identifiers: ISBN 9798384903093 (lib. bdg.) | ISBN 9798384903796 (ebook) | ISBN 9798384904144 (Read-to-me ebook)

Subjects: LCSH: Monkeys--Juvenile literature. | Primates--Juvenile literature. | Rain forest animals --Juvenile literature. | Wildlife--Juvenile literature. | Enigmas--Juvenile literature.

Classification: DDC 599.82--dc23

Table of Contents

Uakari

The uakari is a monkey that is found in South America. It lives in the Amazon River **basin**. It prefers rainforests that flood during the rainy season.

Uakari
Range
South
America

Uakaris gather in large groups called troops. Troops can have up to 200 members. At night, troops stay together high up in trees.

Uakaris are unusual! They have a red, **bald** face. This is because they have thin skin and lots of **blood vessels** in their cheeks and forehead.

Body

Uakaris are the same size as a small house cat. They grow 14 to 20 inches (36 to 51 cm) long. They can weigh 6 to 7.5 pounds (2.7 to 3.4 kg).

Uakaris have long, **shaggy** fur that is reddish brown or orange in color. They have short tails.

Uakaris have long, strong arms and legs. Their fingers and toes are long too! They rely on all of these to move through the trees.

Uakaris walk and run on all four **limbs**. They can also walk and jump on two legs. They jump and bounce from tree to tree.

Food

The uakari mainly eats fruit. It also eats leaves, insects, and roots. Its strong jaws and sharp teeth allow it to easily break open nuts.

Baby Uakaris

Females are pregnant for six months. They give birth to one baby every two years. Babies are born helpless. They rely on their mothers for food and safety.

More Facts

- Uakaris use sounds and **body language** to communicate with each other.
- Uakaris are found in Peru, Brazil, and Colombia.
- The brighter red a uakari's face is, the more attractive it is to a **mate**.

Glossary

bald – having little or no hair.

basin – the area of land drained by a river.

blood vessel – any of the tubes (such as veins and arteries) in the body through which the blood moves.

body language – the shifts of posture, gestures, and facial expressions that communicate nonverbally.

limb – an arm or leg.

mate – one of a pair that come together to have young.

shaggy – having long, rough hair or something like hair.

Index

Visit **abdokids.com** to access crafts, games, videos, and more!

Use Abdo Kids code

UUK3093

or scan this QR code!